The Call of the Kinchafoonie

N Wayne Garrett.
Echohead

Squibbles

Copyright 2016   Kinchafoonie South Publishing

All rights reserved, including the right of reproduction in whole or in part by any means, electronic or mechanical including but not limited to photocopying or recording and strictly prohibited without the written permission of the publisher.

Printed in the United States of America

First Edition

ISBN 13: 978 – 1537222622
ISBN 10: 1537222627

Address inquiries to:

Kinchafoonie South Publishing

P O Box 15902,

Panama City, FL 32406

Dedication

. . . for you, Sug

Squibbles

Squibbles are stories about things I see;
Things that happen and that happen to me;

About writers and poets and the folks who write,
About bugs and beaches and living and life.

Most of my thoughts come out in rhyme,
Perhaps the result of a resonant mind,

Never knowing where to go when it gets started,
Sometimes profound but generally lighthearted.

Come along now and we'll journey through,
And as we go, I'll make a comment or two,

About how this book came to be,
And what in the world is poetry.

Who are writers and why they write,
Tools they need and keeping goals in sight.

We'll add some thoughts about things mundane,
About fishing and mooseing and hurricanes.

Ageing with grace while growing old,
And how memory's reflection soothes the soul.

My efforts will prove to be worthwhile,
If at the end of our journey; you look up and smile.

Index

Writers and Writing

Writing Class	11
Brainy Folk	12
Quest	13
Writing Tools	14
The Writing Life	15
Seminar	16
The Publisher	17
Writers Conference	18
Writer's Conference # 8	19
Due Today	20
Writer's Block	21
Writer!	22

Poems and Poets

Echoheads	24
Short Rows	25
A Posit on Poets	26
Some'n Funny	27
Quandary	28
Quandary Resolved	29
Elideonyms	30
Poems n' Art	32

Bugs and Beaches

My Florida	34
Dragonflies	36
Contemplation	37
Bay Life	38
Boomer's Dream	40
The Trophy	41
City of Panama City	42
Ballard of Cove Pig	44
Mallard in a Mixing Bowl	46
Storms	47

Living and Life

Floors	**49**
Heading Home	**50**
Organizing	**52**
Complicated	**53**
Treasures	**54**
Friend and Roses	**55**
Mooseing Through	**56**
Angie's Address Book	**58**
Flags	**59**
Momma's Kitchen Window	**60**
Some Days	**61**
Inspiration/Motivation	**62**
Aging Grace	**63**
Reflections	**64**
Journey's End	**65**
About the author	**67**

Squibbles

----------*of writers and writing*

Is word weaving innate wizardry,
Allowed to very few?
Or is it a learned craft,
That ordinary folks can do?

Writing Class

For six weeks on the back row,
My mind refused to think.
I could not make my hand go near,
Paper, pen, or ink.

I left it to my classmates,
The entire load to tote,
While I sat like a big old lump,
And never wrote a note.

But I did pay attention,
And I heard some real good stuff,
Like: "You have to keep on learning,
'Cause you never know enough."

"Be yourself" and "Tell the truth,"
"Write the things you know,"
"Careful with the dialog,"
"Let the story flow."

Don't try to be Twain or Tolstoy,
Trollope or Khayyam,
Let your words on paper say,
This is who I am.

And the greatest lesson to be learned,
Came through crystal clear,
Skill and talent aren't enough,
You must persevere!

Brainy Folk

The group 'round me, assembled,
Was a quite eclectic crowd,
A gathering of writers,
With wit and wisdom well endowed.

Purveyors of information,
Possessing word skills to be proud;
"What am I doing sitting here,
With such a brainy crowd?"

My heretofore companions,
Were into other kinds of fun,
Like drinking 'shine around a campfire,
And listening to hound dogs run.

But if everybody liked the same ol' thing,
This world would sure be bland.
That which some folks think is yucky,
To others may be grand.

It ain't wrong, at all, to be different,
It's generally a matter of taste.
And there's room for diverse opinions,
In the scope of the human race.

Don't judge by the outside cover,
Evaluate each one as a whole,
The true merit of a being,
Is in the goodness of their soul.

In that, brainy friends ain't different,
From other chums I've had,
They just talk a whole lot better,
And they sure don't smell as bad.

Quest

I joined a local writer's group,
To learn the latest stuff.
Just getting old don't make you smart,
And you never know enough.

There are tales I want to tell,
That may best be done in prose;
But should I make a sound track?
Leave writing to the pros?

I know folks will laugh,
At my stories when they're heard,
But do they laugh at what I wrote,
Or at how I said the words?

I can judge reaction,
To a quip or to a quote,
But how to know what people think,
When they read the words you wrote?

Sounds you make just dissipate,
Before they're even cold.
But what you put on paper,
Gives a peek into your soul.

The questions are the same,
As they have always been,
Since people scratched clay tablets,
With sharp sticks for a pen.

Can you really open up?
Can you say what's on your mind?
Are the things you have to say,
Worth the reader's time?

When you conquer trepidation,
The answer comes to light.
You have to let folks read your stuff,
To find out if you can write.

Writing Tools

The point of this discussion,
Is useful writing tools.
Does that mean pens and pencils,
And lessons learned in schools?

Perhaps Roget's Thesaurus,
Or Mr. Webster's book,
Those two will steal an afternoon,
If opened for a look.

They've got words I didn't know,
Much less know how to use,
And time flies by like lighting,
When their pages I peruse.

A handy dandy computer,
To type on and to print,
Gadgets, so very helpful,
They must be Heaven sent.

A tool can also be a place,
Instead of just a thing.
Somewhere your heart finds solace,
Or that makes your spirits sing.

Too, we should consider,
Things not so mundane,
Like leaves and clouds and dragonflies,
And gently falling rain.

How about faith as inspiration,
To open up your dreams,
And search for understanding,
Of what life truly means?

Another tool is courage,
To overcome your fears.
But the most essential tool for writing,
Is found between your ears.

The Writing Life

A successful published writer,
Came and spoke to us one night.
He told our group of fledging authors,
All about the "Writing Life."

The group was most attentive,
To every clue and hint.
They shared a common longing,
To see their words in print.

He knew that few would make it,
Despite all effort, it would seem.
Still he offered his assistance,
To help them chase their dream.

He bolstered confidence and courage,
Gave tips and ways "how to,"
A resolve to carry forward,
With the things they want to do..

He brought his son there with him,
A bright and sturdy lad.
Reminded me of taking mine,
Or my travels with my dad.

Just one of many outings,
The youth had ventured to.
He needed no explanation,
Of what he watched his daddy do.

Sharing time and talent,
Helping folks along the way,
An unselfish act of kindness,
Was fully on display.

Learning within learning,
What a stirring sight.
A father, teaching by example,
Another lesson taught that night.

Seminar

I right much enjoyed the meeting,
'Bout how to write a book,
And stood in awe and wonder,
At how much work it took.

It takes more than just a story
That you want to tell
And the fortitude and patience
To really tell it well.

You have to cut and edit
Make sure its fit to print.
And never, never wonder
Where your time and money went.

But you just gotta do it,
In spite of all the fuss,
You don't write because you want to.
You write because you must.

The Publisher

The speaker's voice was smooth and soft,
But clearly could be heard.
The crowd was most attentive,
To her every word.

A publisher had come to talk,
At the local writer's hall,
Eager aspiring authors,
Filled the room from wall to wall.

The group was quite diverse,
Male, female, young, and old.
The desire to see their work in print,
Was their unifying goal.

Some yearn for fame and fortune,
To grasp the golden ring.
Others want to tell the world,
Some important thing.

A few write just to entertain,
Themselves, or all mankind,
Rewarded amply by a laugh,
When they write a funny line.

Each holds a different promise,
And their efforts we salute.
What a dreary world we'd live in,
If writers all were mute.

With no songs to raise our spirits
Would not the door to beauty close?
And our universe be poorer
Sans poetry? Sans prose?

Write on, write on, you writers,
Pursue your dreams with pride.
No matter what your output,
The world is better 'cause you tried.

Writers Conference

From coat and tie to sloppy chic,
A quite eclectic sight,
A polyglot of people,
Whose dream is but to write.

The gathered were the "wanna do's,"
To be published their desire.
They seek that fulfilled promise,
With ambition's burning fire.

Novelists and poets,
And humorist, tongue in cheek,
Each one with a personal goal,
Their own brass ring to seek.

To immerse the world in knowledge,
The next "War and Peace" to craft,
Or maybe write a funny line,
And make somebody laugh.

Listen, learn and persevere,
Edit and promote.
An unread work will not receive,
One Pulitzer vote.

But to each, success is different,
For some, the end is not the mean,
And the outcome's not the ending,
It's enough to live the dream.

Writers Conference # 8

Some came to mingle;
Some to learn,
Some came driven by ambition's burn.

Some dressed up,
Some dressed down,
Some pastel – some, earthy brown.

Some came early,
Some came late.
Some were anxious, some just wait.

Some to bolster,
Some to lean,
Some to strive; some to dream.

Some will grasp golden rings,
Some will settle for lesser things.

All shall learn that in the end,
Those who try are those who win.

Due Today

It's already too late thirty,
And I'm wondering what to do.
Should I show up empty handed,
With an excuse or two?

Ought I toss some lines together?
Pretend I really tried?
Knowing it is not my best,
Just take an easy slide.

I really have been busy,
But I would have to say,
Things put off until tomorrow,
Could have been handled yesterday.

We all live on borrowed time,
Not knowing when the note comes due.
So, there are things to think about,
And things we need to do.

Pass out your roses every day,
Wisely spend your time,
Discipline and dedication,
Will help you toe the line.

Keep your eyes on the horizon,
With goals foremost on your mind,
Avoid procrastination,
That subtle thief of time.

Set aside moments for joy and love,
For mirth and foolish stuff,
But keep in mind; when it comes to time,
There never is enough.

Writer's Block

Have you ever had a time,
When your mind goes on the blink,
When your prose don't make a lick of sense,
And the poems you write just stink?

Do you blame it on the weather?
And wait for a better time,
Or ask yourself the question
Could the fault be really mine?

Maybe you have lost your touch
Or said all you had to say,
Perhaps a life of silent solitude,
Would be a better way?

But then, that isn't likely,
You are not that kind of nut,
The one thing you can't do for long,
Is keep your big mouth shut.

Writer!

Oh! To be a writer,
What an endless thrill!
Spinning worlds of imagination,
With words from a magic quill.

Relating flights of fantasy,
In a universe unbound,
Away in space, far out at sea,
Or deep in the underground.

Tales of epic adventure,
Sagas of the inner soul,
Stories of love and yearning,
Or quests for hidden gold.

The subject lines are endless,
The plots, a million-fold,
An ever changing litany,
Of stories to be told.

If you would be a writer,
And seek that unique thrill,
Preen your imagination,
And hone your writing skill.

Let your stories freely flow,
And make your meaning clear,
Keep readers foremost in your mind,
And in your efforts, persevere.

----------*of poems and poets*

Why are some writers poets?
Why do they spend their time,
Racking their brains searching for ways,
To express their thoughts in rhyme?

Echoheads

Thoughts reverberate inside my head,
And bounce around sometime,
And when they reach my fingers,
The lines I write all rhyme.

Does that make me a poet?
That's what I'd like to know,
So when the invitation came,
I really had to go.

There was planned a gathering,
Where poets would surely be,
In the great storehouse of knowledge,
Down by the Emerald Sea.

For answers to my questions,
I would go and ask the best.
They have poetic license,
So they must have passed a test.

Are poets mighty muses,
With long goatees and such;
Screen saver eyes like pools of dreams,
Too deep and dark to touch?

Is word weaving innate wizardry,
Allowed to very few?
Or is it a learned craft,
That ordinary folks can do?

The answer's no more complex,
Than noses on a face
There are lots of different kinds,
But each one has a place.

Some poems flow from the magic pens,
Of spirits that are free.
While others are the just the gleeful work,
Of an Echohead, like me.

Short Rows

When you're living life in the short rows,
You need to allocate your time.
Should you spend it trying to create prose,
Or just play around with rhyme?

To those of the writing avocation,
Devotees of the language art,
Poems are rather mundane things,
Prose is the highbrow part.

Aside from being proper,
Prose follows all the rules,
'Bout grammar, 'n spelling 'n English stuff,
They teach about in schools.

Broad reference is a no-no,
Sentence fragment or comma splice,
Dangling participle, split infinitive,
None of those things are nice.

Beware those devious adverbs,
Keep constantly on your toes,
Or they'll be slurping, most stealthily,
The vitality from your prose.

Watch out for prepositions.
Don't you dare to forget about that.
In your prose, don't use too many of them,
And be careful where you put 'em at.

But poems can sort of find their way,
With a personality of their own,
Just make them sound like you want 'em to,
And let the subject set the tone.

I salute those who write for the ages,
Whose words stand the test of time,
But I'll concentrate on simple things,
And express my thoughts in rhyme.

I may never write deathless prose,
But maybe I can cause a smile.
If I can brighten someone's day,
My time is spent worthwhile.

A Posit on Poets

Do you wonder why people want to be poets?
Or why they spend their time,
Racking their brains searching for ways,
To express their thoughts in rhyme?

Are they beset by Muses,
Who whisper in dreams at night,
"Use the language like a paint brush,
Animate the things you write"?

Is poetry an innate talent,
Or a studied, learned craft?
Are poets the wizards of the written word,
Or writers who are slightly daft?

Why are they always driven,
When picking up pen and ink
Not only to try to make you laugh or cry
But to try to make you think.

With a song to elate the spirit,
Or an ode to soothe a soul,
In their own way make a difference,
A small, but noble goal.

Or, perhaps, the really, real reason
That poetry's their avocation,
Is an undomesticated lagomorph,
In their solar deprived location.

Some'n Funny

Can you write some'n funny on purpose?
Pen laughter right out of the air,
Get grins by scribing intelligent stuff,
Like "Hot dang, you all, I swear?"

Is it possible to print out a snicker?
Word picture a groaning guffaw,
Tell a funny bone, it's tickled,
Scribble smiles from your mother in law?

Will words on paper cause laughter?
Manufacture some chuckles and grins,
By journalizing our foibles,
Making light of our virtues and sins.

Think back to the very beginning,
The origin of the species stuff.
The rumor is the good Lord made us,
Because the monkeys weren't funny enough.

So keep your quill on the sunny side,
Don't post a squally ol' mope.
And good cheer will always surround you,
Because the flip side of humor is hope.

Quandary

The question, thru the ages,
Asked, from time to time:
Can it really be a poem,
If the couplets do not rhyme?

Must there be a lyric,
With melodic sound,
Or could it be in rhythm,
That poetry is found?

Must a poem sing like a song,
Or may it read like prose?
Is a magnolia less than lovely,
Because it's different from a rose?

The answer is in diversity,
For each style has a place.
Rhyme gives our language music,
Free verse reflects its grace.

Quandary Resolved

When dealing with proponents,
Of blank verse or of rhyme.
The keys to understanding,
Are difficult to find.

Are free versers etherealist,
Who think outside the box?
Is there a rhyming poet,
Under every rock?

Is rhyming verse like candy,
Sticky to the ear?
Must you write in free verse,
To make your meaning clear?

The Guru of the Ages,
Revealed the answer, short and frank:
"Some poets' minds think in rhymes,
Other poets' minds are blank."

Elideonyms

Anonyms mean the opposite.
Synonyms: Same meaning; different word.
Homonyms all sound alike.
Elideonyms are slurred.

They are multi-word expressions,
Condensed to a single word,
That looks one way when you write it
And another way when it's heard.

Of examples, there are many.
We use them every day,
With no thought the words we're reading,
Are not the words we say.

"A'punce", "an'nym", and "fi'si'di",
Are three that come to mind,
And "ya'hyr" and "je'et" are elideonyms,
You hear all the time.

"A'punce" starts all our fairy tales,
Like: Once a'punce (upon a) time,
And "an'nym" is all the kith and kin,
That someone left behind.

The old standard Southern greeting
"Hi y'all – how you been?
Gosh, it's good to see you,
How's your mama an'nym (and them)?"

"Je'et" shows a friendly concern,
Of whether you have dined today
Instead of asking, "Have you had supper?"
"Je'et" is what we say"

Elideonyms

Ya'hyr" asks if your ears work,
"Are you listening to me?"
The Yankee elideonym version ,
Is pronounced "Ya'see."

It concludes the sentence,
Inquires if the meaning's clear,
Did you understand what I told you?
"Y'all come see us now ya'hyr (you hear?)?"

"Fi'si'di" comes at evening time,
"Now, I lay me down to sleep,
Fi'si'di (if I should die) before I wake.
I pray the Lord, my soul to keep."

And when you are talking to your Maker,
Everything you say,
Is understood, no matter the words,
When you open your heart to pray.

Poems n' Art

Are poems the gems of the language art?

Shiny baubles set apart;
To fill a niche and add their gleams,
To discourse oft bereft of dreams.

Are poems the spice of the language art?

Zip and zest that sets apart;
Thoughts to savor; ideals to soar,
A chant to ease a boring chore.

Are poems the tools of the language art?

Devices used to set apart;
Thoughtful pondering, renewal of hope,
Cause a smile or a catch in the throat.

Are poems the soul of language art?

Linguistic essence set apart;
The lift and lilt; to laugh and sing,
Joy and wonder, remembering.

Are poems essential to the language art?

A necessary genre set apart;
For useful musings or amusing fluff,
Word cotton candy or important stuff.

The answer is quite very easy to see,
They are, what they are,
Perceived to be.

----------*of bugs and beaches*

Yes, my Florida is changing
And her future is up to us,
To preserve our living heritage,
Is our most enduring trust.

My Florida

I went to see my Florida,
One more time today,
To burn her image in my brain,
Before she fades away.

To the last place on the water's edge,
To stand in pre-dawn light,
On pristine dunes that stretch away,
Not another soul in sight.

To hear the quiet murmur,
Of gulf waves rolling in,
And watch a flight of pelicans,
Hang motionless on the wind.

As seagulls shriek "Good Morning,"
To the sandpipers running by,
I strain my ears to listen,
For the panther's lonely cry.

A gator bellows from the dune lake,
To greet the rising sun,
As raccoons scurry homeward,
From their early morning run.

I went to see my Florida,
One more time today,
I'd like to keep her as she is,
But that's not for me to say.

My Florida

Making room for others,
Is changing her, you see,
But not so very long ago,
She made a place for me

If we hoard the things we love,
Tight - bundled, close and dry,
Hidden from view, away from the sun,
They wither up and die.

The way to truly keep things,
Is to open up and share.
And with others be good stewards,
Mix common sense with care,

Yes, my Florida is changing,
And her future's up to us,
To preserve our living heritage,
Is our most enduring trust.

And we can have our Florida,
Both the old and new.
Because what the future holds for her,
Is up to me and you.

Dragonflies

I sat at my window,
My fist beneath my chin,
Watching dragonflies flit about,
Like darters on the wind.

Dragonflies of different sizes,
Many colors too,
Shimmering, shining, golden greens,
And iridescent blue.

They are large of head and body,
And strong upon the wing,
All their tails are pointed,
But none contain a sting.

They fly in celebration,
Of their generation's goal,
And at the culmination,
Another will unfold.

They have come full circle,
A new cycle to begin,
Both an ending and beginning,
Is their dance upon the wind.

Contemplation

I watched a spider repair her web,
In the golden predawn light,
And butterflies kiss the honeysuckle,
As they made their morning flight.

The ligustrum hedge was all abuzz,
With bees from hives nearby,
Busily creating honey trails,
As they convoy through the sky

The ants marched forth their aphid herd,
To feed upon the rose,
And I wondered if a thousand leg bug,
Really has five thousand toes?

If there are centipedes and millipedes,
Are there other "pedes" in between?
Why does dragonfly have a pointy tail,
When it doesn't have a sting?

But the most puzzling of my questions,
I would have to say, is:
"Have I been contemplating nature?
Or just watching bugs all day?"

Bay Life

Early in the morning,
We greeted the rising sun,
Rolling through South Georgia,
Our new '46 Ford could run.

World War Two was over,
The struggle had been won,
The country was getting back to normal,
Time to have some fun.

A vacation in Panama City,
That's just the place to be,
Where the "World's Most Beautiful Beaches,"
Make the Gulf, an emerald sea.

That trip marked the beginning,
Of many a pleasant time,
Names and places through the years,
Flow gently across my mind.

Remember the bridge at Lynn Haven,
The old one made of wood,
The planks weren't flying up behind you,
But they sounded like they could.

The old Long Beach Casino,
With its Hangout right nearby,
Captain Anderson's: "Watch the fleet unload,
Fresh caught fish to fry."

The arcade across from Peek's Motel,
Soft serve ice cream cone,
Stop by "Little Birmingham,"
Before you go back home.

Ocean Opry, Petticoat Junction,
Wild and Wet - Slip and Slide,
Goofy Golf, Shipwreck Island,
And one more go – cart ride.

Bay Life

Catching crabs at Mexico Beach,
Cooking 'em on the shore,
Hook a big bass on Deerpoint Lake,
Oh! To do that once more

St Andrew Marina at sunset,
Pelicans flying single file,
While across the bay, construction cranes
Roost on "The Miracle Mile."

Pineapple Willie's and Schooner's,
Spinnaker going strong,
But Canopies and Breakers,
Soon to be long gone.

As old favorites disappear,
New things make their mark,
Like an airport out in the boonies,
And the place they call "Pier Park."

The Titanic sinking on Front Beach Road,
Big Gus is now a steer,
Spring Breakers come down in droves
While a blimp overhead sells beer.

The cool of the condo canyons,
Where it is twilight time at noon,
And jackhammers mounted on backhoes,
Play mariachi tunes.

The old and new meld together,
In a continuing tapestry,
And for the folks who live here,
There's no place they'd rather be.

With glitter and glitz,
And cheese for your grits
All within your reach,
To sum it up best, we can attest:
Bay Life living is a beach.

Boomer's Dream

Soaring towers line the sky,
Hordes of people scurry by,
The noise, the clamor, the city smell,
The cloying boredom of an urban hell,

The work-a day world where the daily grind,
Dulls the senses and numbs the mind,
But made worthwhile if someday to be,
In a tranquil haven by the sea.

A live oak hammock, in shade all day,
Where woodland creatures live and play.
Where seabirds nest and ospreys prey,
From the tallest trees along the bay.

Work and dream, someday we'll be,
In our haven by the sea.
It's almost perfect; yes indeed,
But change must come to fit our need.

Unruly vines; they must go,
And all that brush growing low,
What of the creatures living there?
Where they go is not our care.

Build a place our cars to park,
Put in lights to chase the dark,
A dock and a pier are needed too.
Cut down those trees. They spoil the view.

One thing was left for all to see,
Of how their haven used to be,
One sad Live Oak, standing free,
Alone, amidst an asphalt sea.

They changed it all for comfort sake,
No thought of the difference change would make.
Then through her tears, she softly said,
"We've made it into the place we fled."

The Trophy

It was a perfect afternoon,
To take the bateau out,
In the bay, just waiting for him,
Was a world record speckled trout.

He caught his quarry's little brother,
And threw him right back in,
Baited up his hook once more,
And cast it out again.

His line made a graceful arc,
Flying through the air,
Then he saw something in the water,
With no business being there.

A big black Lab, swimming strong,
But way too far at sea,
The salt had crusted up its eyes,
The poor dog could not see.

It swam in a circle,
Stopped, then swam some more.
It was apparent that brave animal,
Could not find the shore.

"I'll fish no more today," he said,
As he hauled the canine in,,
And proceeded to help a grateful dog,
Find its home again.

In a way we all are fishing,
As we go down our life's path.
We never know what we may catch,
When we make a cast.

But perhaps the finest trophy,
That can be caught, indeed,
Is a chance to help a fellow creature,
That finds itself in need.

City of Panama City
aka
The Bogus Lighthouse Blues
A parody of Arlo Guthrie's *City of New Orleans*

Riding on the highway, to the coastline,
231 from Dothan, don't you know?
Heading for fun, down there in the sunshine,
Rolling south, looking for a place to go.

Good morning, Panama City, how are you?
Don't you know me?
I'm the made up one.
The light house that never was a lighthouse,
But if you build me, surely they will come.

On their tourist odyssey,
The folks come down the sights to see,
Peanut patches, cotton fields and farms,
Passing by the crawdad pond,
Looking for beaches and beyond,
Spending dollars everywhere they go.

But once they get out to the beach,
They are out of downtown reach,
And all that money tends to stay out there.
Spending cash dawn till dark,
Miracle Mile to Pier Park,
Lots of ways to spend up all their dough.

City of Panama City

Good morning, Panama City, how are you?
Don't you know me?
I'm the made up one.
The light house that never was a lighthouse,
But if you build me, surely they will come.

And though downtown's off the beaten path,
And some folks will guffaw and laugh,
The DIB widely spreads the news,
Come over here, one and all,
Y'all can really have a ball,
Rock and roll to the Bogus Lighthouse Blues!

Good morning, Panama City, how are you?
Don't you know me?
I'm the made up one.
The light house that never was a lighthouse,
But if you build me; surely they will come…

Build me -surely they will come??

Surely?

Surely, please?

Build meeee. . . .

Ballard of Cove Pig

Don't haze him, don't taze him,
Don't tempt him with doughnuts.
Leave him alone to roam wild and free.
Don't try to pen up the noblest of creatures,
The greatest Cove Pig you ever did see.

Old Florida is fading, our coast disappearing,
Behind towers of concrete as tall as can be,
We think the beach is still right behind 'em,
But when we ride by, we no longer can see.

The airport is moving out to the boonies,
Condos are empty, the hammers are still,
Are the good times all over? Can they come back?
Dare we to hope and to pray that they will?

Then came a sign, right out of nowhere,
To show us what courage in living's about,
An unlikely hero shrouded in mystery,
From the curl of his tail to the tip of his snout

Don't haze him, don't taze him,
Don't tempt him with doughnuts,
Leave him alone to live wild and free.
Don't try to tame the noblest of creatures,
The greatest Cove Pig you ever did see.

Ballard of Cove Pig

He's a will o' the wisp of porker proportions,
The essence of freedom; how life oughta be,
Stand on your own - no challenge too daunting,
Cope with your troubles 'cause freedom ain't free.

Cove Pig is the spirit that flows in us all,
That makes us pursue the best we can be,
As long as we dream and work toward the future,
His legend lives on through you and through me.

Don't haze him, don't taze him,
Don't tempt him with doughnuts,
Leave him alone to live wild and free
Make a place in your heart for the noblest of creatures,
The greatest Cove Pig there ever will be.

Mallard in a Mixing Bowl

A mallard in a cast off bowl,
A strange, but lovely sight.
The bowl was the ocean's cobalt blue,
The mallard, scarlet, green and white.

Why would a creature of open sky,
Of far flung lake and sea,
Be nestled in a tiny bowl,
As cozy as can be?

Is traversing endless vistas,
Boldly flying free,
Not the all and everything,
Of what a life should be?

Too, is needed sanctuary,
What home and hearth can mean,
A place to settle in safe harbor,
To reflect, perhaps, to dream.

Storms

Far out in the Doldrums,
In seas, dead calm and warm,
Two raindrops and a wisp of wind,
Unite to start a storm.

The wisp becomes a zephyr,
Gathering breezes in a crowd,
The raindrops blithely multiply,
And form a thundercloud.

The winds join hands and circle up,
To begin their fateful dance.
The rain clouds choose their partners,
For the long westward advance.

Gaining scope and power,
Adding bands of wind and rain,
The two drops and the wisp of wind,
Become a hurricane.

Man can choose to hunker down,
Board up or run away.
But he can't affect the outcome,
When the cyclone comes his way.

We view the world from selfish ends,
And get in nature's way,
But storms have different goals in mind,
For the forces they display.

Rain to nourish estuaries,
And help to scrub them clean.
Winds to comb the dead wood out,
Leave the forest clear and green.

The way it is and always was,
Despite our fret and fuss,
Nature's taking care of business,
As it should and as it must.

----------*of living and life*

Truly - being useful,
Makes living life worthwhile.
Don't have to do no big things,
Just make somebody smile.

Floors

You get a different view of things,
When you are sitting on the floor.
A cobweb on a kitchen chair,
You never saw before.

A box beneath the sofa.
How did that get there?
A little bit of ribbon,
Nestled against a chair.

Cords along the wall,
Their tangle is a fright.
But they are all tucked away,
Safely out of sight.

From standing up, it all looks fine,
Everything in place.
Color matched, coordinated,
With a sense of style and grace.

Is the top view just illusion,
For all the world to see,
Or is the underneath,
The true reality?

The answer is that both apply,
Like the ups and downs of life.
The joy and fulfillment,
The struggles and the strife.

The hard parts you don't talk about,
Good things, display with pride.
The under says life ain't easy,
The top side shows you tried.

Heading Home

Well, I cranked her up,
She purred like a cat,
Put her in gear and that was that,
Me and my little truck were headed home.

We'd had it with that Atlanta place,
It's got style,
But lost its grace,
Me and my little truck are going home.

We were feeling good just being alive,
Rolling North off 285,
Cleared Marietta,
Turned west and by passed Rome.

Through Cave Springs, then Mentone,
Over Lookout Mountain in the foggy dawn,
Crossing North Alabama,
And thinking 'bout nothing but home.

We'd been gone too long of a time,
Looking for things we never did find,
But we always knew that one day,
We'd head home.

Then there was the sight,
We were longing to see,
The city limit sign said *Boligee*,
Me and my little truck had made it home.

We pulled down a quiet street,
I laid right over and slept in the seat,
Dreaming sweet dreams,
'Cause we was finally home.

Heading Home

Up next morning at the crack of dawn,
Looking for the things I'd missed so long,
And to let the town folks know,
That I was home.

But nothing was where it was supposed to be,
And nobody ever heard of me,
They just shook their heads and said,
"You been gone how long?"

It was the same,
But a different place,
Might as well been in outer space,
The hometown of my childhood days was gone.

So all you ramblers listen here,
You better hug the things that you hold dear,
Keep in touch,
And don't stay away too long.

Or you will suffer our sorry fate,
You'll mess around and wait too late,
And have nowhere to go,
When you head home.

Heading home, heading home,
Me & my little truck ain't got no home.

Organize'n

Before laughing at all my clutter,
And judging me, perhaps, in haste,
Remember I live in a throwaway world,
But taught from childhood not to waste.

Use it up and fix it,
Save it for another time,
Never know when you might need one,
Things like that are hard to find.

Then, the realization hits you,
"What's this world a' coming to?
It costs more to fix the old one,
Than buy another that's brand new."

Do you need all this accumulation?
So much assorted stuff?
Don't you know just looking around,
You have more than enough?

Now, don't let greed bring visions,
Of gleaming antique gold,
Because aging junk don't make it treasure,
Aging junk just makes it old.

So get yourself to organizing,
And make the bold assumption:
You can have a neater life,
If you just get up the gumption.

Complicated

Why is life so busy?
Why so much to do?
Seems like 'fore you finish up,
You got to start on somethin' new.

The work just don't get over,
And there ain't no quitting time.
No matter how you hurry up,
You still stay way behind.

But truly - being useful,
Makes living life worthwhile.
Don't have to do no big things,
Just make somebody smile.

Lend a hand in helping others,
Be kind to someone every day,
Spread a little joy and sunshine,
As you go along the way.

Don't let yourself get in a rut,
You know what that's about.
A rut is just a big ol' grave,
With both the ends knocked out.

Be glad you can contribute,
And do so every day,
Leave the path a little brighter,
For those who come your way.

You don't know how long you'll be here,
But while you're still on hand,
Make the best of what you are given,
Be a boon to your fellow man.

Treasures

The laughter of children,
The coo of a dove,
Looks people share,
When they are truly in love.

The gift of a greeting,
The joy of a grin
Wrinkles on faces
Where smiles have been.

The gold of the sky
At dawn's early light
The shine of a star
In the purple of night.

The smell of the sea breeze
When it crosses the land
A drawing in crayon
Made by a small hand.

The true treasures of life,
As you can see,
Are not things you can buy,
They are things that are free.

Friends and Roses

In splendid, simple beauty
There stands alone, the rose
Object of the poet's rhyme,
Glorified in prose.

Blossoms tightly budded,
Amid the leaves and thorn,
Conceal resplendent glory,
Waiting to be born.

As it unfurls its petals,
The lovelier it grows,
Until revealed in splendor,
Is the perfect rose.

Roses grow in rocky soil,
And in the fertile loam,
The bloom can be as lovely,
No matter which is home.

There is required a nurture,
To make them look so grand,
And like the rose, each of us,
Needs a caring hand.

A smile, a word, a gentle touch,
A heartfelt, "How are you?"
Someone to listen to your woe,
And share your laughter too.

Friends and roses need attention,
Well worth the time you spend,
As precious as a perfect rose,
Are those who call you friend.

Mooseing Thru

When age weighs down upon you
And your parts start coming loose,
It's kinda hard to deal with,
When you used to be a Moose.

Being a Moose didn't make you special,
It was just a way to do.
Confronted with a problem,
You'd just go Mooseing through.

Dig in your toes, lower your head,
Take a three-point stance
Drive straight into the challenge,
Trouble didn't stand a chance.

And if your Mooseing didn't work,
You could still be proud,
To survive the situation,
Bloody, but unbowed.

But, "Pride goeth before destruction
And a haughty spirit before the fall"
Infirmity and limitation,
Is the fate that awaits us all.

Still you rise to the occasion,
But just not as quick.
It takes a while to get there,
When you are walking with a stick.

Mooseing Thru

Got to find your glasses,
Switch on your electric ear.
Careful not to talk too much,
'Till you get your brain in gear.

Learn to put aside your vanity,
Let others help you through.
Using brains instead of brawn,
Is a way of Mooseing, too.

Count your blessings when you wake up.
Do a kindness every day.
Spread a little sunshine,
As you go along the way.

Success in its true merit
Is not how slick a race you ran,
The real deciding factor,
Is how you treat your fellow man.

Angie's Address Book

In the corner of her roll-top desk,
In a little hidden nook,
She found an item, long misplaced,
A dusty old address book.

On its dog eared pages,
Names of dear old friends,
The places where they used to be,
And the numbers they had then.

As pages turned, stories came,
Joy, laughter, and some tears,
Friends and neighbors came to mind,
Not thought about for years.

She never left her desk that day,
But what a trip she took,
A wonderful stroll down memory lane,
Through that nondescript little brown book.

Flags

Tiny flags adorn the roadway,
Snapping proudly in the breeze.
There is bunting on the houses,
Yellow ribbons in the trees.

There are smiles on all the faces,
Our troops are coming back.
They've been half the world away,
In the deserts of Iraq.

They went when duty called them,
As others have before,
To keep Old Glory flying,
And the tyrant from our shore.

Like the Minutemen and Doughboys,
They've been serving Uncle Sam,
As did G. I. Joe, the Roughriders,
And the Grunts in Viet Nam.

Throughout our nation's history,
Generations heed the call,
Stepping forward bravely,
Our finest standing tall.

There is a price for freedom,
And the toll will always be,
Paid in blood and courage,
By those who keep us free.

So play the music proudly,
Put flags along the way,
Today, our troops are coming home.
God bless the U S A.

Momma's Kitchen Window

When sunbeams kissed her window crystals,
They sent rainbows everywhere.
Scattered across the counter,
On the kitchen chair.

In the palm of Momma's hand,
Another in her hair.
"Catch one on your tongue and taste it."
Rainbows everywhere.

Rainbows for your fingers,
Rainbows on your clothes.
On a floor strewn with rainbows,
They dance upon your toes.

When the world wears down upon me,
And I need find peace and calm.
I relive those magic moments,
Catching rainbows,
With my mom.

Some Days

Some days are better than others,
But it's good to have a day at all,
Be it a nice, crisp spring morning,
Or a leaf crunchy day in the fall.

A tooth chattering spell in the winter,
Doesn't give me a second thought,
Or a chin dripping dog day in summer
When sitting in the shade gets hot.

Just the pleasure of being here,
Is mighty fine by me,
I want to hang around long as I can,
And see what there is to see.

I like being aboard life's carrousel,
Just to be in the saddle and ride,
Maybe I won't grab a big brass ring,
But, at least, I'll know I tried.

There are all kinds of nooks and crannies,
In what this life's about
You can tackle it all with a big ol' smile,
Or with your bottom lip poked out.

In the end, the outcome's just the same,
To a sad or a happy race.
The difference is the route we choose,
And how we set the pace.

In this bed of roses,
To which all of us are born,
There are lots of pretty flowers,
And all the stems have thorns.

You can gaze at the beauty,
Smell the aroma contained therein,
Or sit right down upon them,
And use your other end.

The approach we take is up to us,
A worried frown or a cheerful grin,
But choose the way you go with care,
'Cause you won't come around again.

Inspiration/Motivation
(Revisiting an Aesop fable)

When the hound dog saw the hare run by,
He had an inspired thought.
"That rabbit could be my supper tonight,
If he can just be caught."

The chase was on across the fields,
Through woods, both thin and dense.
They ran right by an old farmer,
Sitting on a round rail fence.

Through the briar patch, across the bog,
It would be the bunny's day
He found a hole in the big stone wall,
And wriggled clean away.

The dog went back by the farmer,
With his head kinda hanging down.
"That rabbit plum' outslickered you,
You sure ain't much of a hound."

"Consider the motivation," Dog replied,
"In our little bit of strife."
"I was running for some dinner,
He was running for his life."

The lesson in this old story,
Is a very important one.
Inspiration gets the job going,
Motivation gets it done.

Aging Grace

Thoughtful folks pontificate,
'Bout growing old with grace,
But none of their lines of rhetoric,
Mention lines etched in your face.

Aging gracefully has a cozy sound,
Like waltzing in the rain,
But with one hand on your partner,
And the other hand on your cane.

Viewing life's ballroom thru bi-focals,
With a stereo hearing aid,
Tripping the "Light Fantastic,"
Becomes a three point promenade.

Picture Charlton Heston playing Moses,
I thought I'd look like him,
But my mirror shows: Red Skelton's,
Kiddlehopper- Klem.

But it's not really about how you look,
It's the way you act and feel.
Pecan pie is mighty good,
Even when your teeth aren't real.

Grace is how you mellow out,
And treat your fellow man.
How you view the world around you,
And contribute what you can.

Just being here is pretty good,
Counting blessings all the while,
Be kind to someone every day,
And show the world a smile.

Reflections

There is a time in every life,
When sadness comes to call,
When the taste of golden sweetness,
Gives way to bitter gall.

Awash in waves of sorrow,
Teardrop torrents flow.
Darkness of despair descends,
The world seems endless woe.

Standing on the edge,
Of sorrow's abysmal pit,
Asking, where, in life's great puzzle,
Do these broken pieces fit?

Then memory's reflections,
Like tiny rays of light,
Penetrate the darkness,
Like fireflies in the night.

Thoughts of all the good times,
Blessings you have had,
For so much to be thankful,
So little that was sad.

Hope returns your courage.
Faith renews your soul.
The caring of your loved ones,
Drives away the cold.

Dawn breaks apart the darkness,
The cycle to complete.
It takes a bite of bitter,
To know how precious is the sweet.

*"We have reached our journey's end,
With one last thought to file.*

*Thank you for the time you spent.
I hope you found a smile."*

* * * * * * *   *
* *

About the author:

Wayne Garrett lives in the Boonies by the Bay, Bay County, Panama City Florida.

Squibbles is his third book and the first collection of poems to be published. A second collection of poems, and a collection of stories, *Beautiful View* will be available in early 2017.

His book, *The Last of the Horse and Buggy Country Doctors*, is currently available on Amazon.

A number of his short stories and poems have been published in regional, local and on-line publications. He is a member of the Panama City Writers, The Florida Storytellers Association and is one of the Bay Storytellers.
.
None of his writings would likely have been published if not for a promise made a long time ago to a magic lady - Mrs. Margie Harris of Buena Vista, Georgia. A promise not to let the stories fade away when he does.

Credit also due to all the folks who made kind comments about poems released over the years and encouraged hard copy publication. A special nod to Mark Boss and Pat Hall for their assistance and suggestions on this volume.

* * * * * * * *
* *

Made in the USA
Charleston, SC
08 December 2016